Your
Grieving
Child

Answers to Questions on Death and Dying

Your Grieving Child

Bill Dodds

Our Sunday Visitor Publishing Division
Our Sunday Visitor, Inc.
Huntington, Indiana 46750

The publisher and author are grateful to those copyright holders (mentioned in the Sources) whose material has been adapted in one manner or another and used in this book. Every reasonable effort has been made to determine copyright holders. If any copyrighted materials have been inadvertently used in this work without proper credit being given in one form or another, please notify Our Sunday Visitor in writing so that future printings of this work may be corrected accordingly.

Our Sunday Visitor Publishing Division
Our Sunday Visitor, Inc.
200 Noll Plaza
Huntington, IN 46750

ISBN: 0-87973-398-5
LCCCN: 00-140006

Cover design by Monica Haneline
PRINTED IN THE UNITED STATES OF AMERICA

In loving memory of my great-nephew
Carsten Cole Buckley
*(April 27, 1999 * May 19, 2000)*

Table of Contents

Introduction:
Finding the Words

Every parent knows children ask hard questions. Sometimes it's difficult to find the right words — the right way — to answer. That can be especially true following the death of a loved one.

This book wasn't written to be read cover to cover. It was designed to help you answer your children's questions about death and dying. Its purpose is to help them — and you — through the difficult time your family is facing. It's a time that many families discover can also be deeply spiritual.

The answers are only suggestions. No one knows your child better than you do. No one is more qualified to adapt and paraphrase the words to best meet his or her needs.

Then, too, by looking over the questions here, you may have a better idea of what your child would like to ask but hasn't been able to. And your teen may want to simply be given the book and the opportunity to examine it alone.

I'm not a professional grief counselor. I'm a fellow parent who has held his son, who has hugged his daughter, as tears flowed and I fumbled for words. I'm a fellow parent who has learned that sometimes the only answer for a grieving child is to hold or hug that child, quietly, wordlessly, lovingly.

Obviously, I don't know your name or your particular situation, but you have been on my mind as I wrote this book. You have been in my prayers.

BILL DODDS

I

Grief: The Basics

Grief isn't a single emotion. It involves a host of feelings and raises a host of concerns, fears, and questions. For anyone at any age.

These days it's commonly accepted that there's a "cycle of grief." There are pieces or periods of the grieving process. But those pieces, those periods, don't necessarily follow a set pattern or stick to a particular time frame. And even after having "gone through" one part, the person who is grieving may — time and again — return to that aspect of grief.

How one grieves, just as how one lives and how one loves, is unique for each individual. Just as each child has a particular personality, each may experience grief in a different way with different questions, even within the same family.

With that in mind, it sometimes helps to understand that within the "cycle" there are four sections:

• Shock and denial. Your son just can't — just won't — believe this has happened. He hopes perhaps it's all only a bad dream. During this time, he feels confused. Later, he may not remember some of the things he said or did. He may ask the same question or set of questions several times.

• Anger and guilt. Your daughter is mad at Grandpa for dying and leaving the family. For leaving her. She's mad at you. Mad at God. Mad at the doctor or hospital staff. At the same time she feels guilty, believing that — somehow, in some way — this is partly her fault.

Then, too — for an older child — if the death

16

followed a chronic illness, he may feel even worse because a part of him may be glad the ordeal is over. During this stage of grief, others around him may seem so stupid. Their concerns so petty.

• Depression. Your child may realize that there are no completely satisfactory nor completely satisfying answers to explain what has happened. She feels so lonely. And she's so tired.

• Adjustment or acceptance. At this point your son may notice he's starting to bounce back. Starting to play and laugh again. But with that can come feelings of disloyalty to the loved one who has died. Somehow his moving on is a betrayal.

Elisabeth Kübler-Ross, a pioneer in bereavement ministry and author of *On Death and Dying*, adds one more section. In the middle she includes bargaining. If your daughter promises to be very, very good, no one else she loves will die. If she vows to be perfect, maybe all of this is some kind of mix-up or mistake and that particular friend or family member isn't really dead.

What can you expect from your child if he or she is grieving? (Or if you're going through grief?) It is an extremely stressful time. That wide, multi-layered range of emotions can be constantly shifting.

Your child's anger, loneliness, sense of loss, and even physical pain can be triggered by any number of things. By realizing Grandpa's favorite television program is about to start. By even thinking about Christmas without Mom. By hearing a joke or having a story from school that would have amused her sibling.

By catching a whiff of aftershave. By smelling bacon cooking. By holding that loved one's hair-brush or hammer. By so many things your son or daughter sees or hears or touches or tastes or feels.

In grief's early stages it's not uncommon to feel anxious and vulnerable. To feel ill. There may be a tightness in the chest and throat. Headaches. Fatigue. Stomach problems.

You daughter may not be able to eat. May not be able to sleep or can't seem to do anything but sleep. May not be able to stop crying. May worry that she's going crazy.

Your son may withdraw socially. May want to be alone. May become more dependent on another family member. May cling to you like he did when he was very small.

What can you do to help your child if he or she is grieving? (What can you do to help yourself?) These are some points to consider:

• How each person grieves is unique. A child shouldn't compare how she grieves, or feels the need to grieve, with anyone else's method. The best way for her is whatever works best for her.

• Your son needs to eat properly and get enough sleep (or at least rest), even if he doesn't feel like doing either.

• It may help if your daughter "works" on her grief. If, when a feeling surfaces, she doesn't automatically push it aside. If she lets herself cry when

18

she feels the need to cry, to get angry when she feels mad, and so on.

• This can be an incredibly spiritual time in his or her life. And in yours. Encourage your child to turn to God.

• Your child may benefit from counseling. A therapist or grief minister can't take away the pain but, at times, can help make it more bearable. Can help make it easier to understand why he or she is feeling all those jumbled feelings.

• Encourage your child, when the time is right, to consider having his or her own ritual for saying good-bye. Maybe it's visiting the grave site alone (while you wait in the car). Maybe "writing a letter" to the loved one who has died. It's doing whatever it is that "fits" him or her, that fits them, best.

It shouldn't be surprising that your child may feel a need for a private and personal memorial. The earthly relationship the two of them shared was one of a kind, too. It was irreplaceable.

II

The

Big

Questions

1
Why did she have to die?

Death is a part of life. It's the end of life on earth. Some people die when they're very young and some die when they're very old. Sometimes a person's body just wears out after a long, long time and sometimes a person's body simply gets sick or gets hurt or has something wrong with it and it just can't keep going.

We never know how long someone will live, but when she does die, we feel very sad. It's like she went on a trip and she left us behind. We love her very much and so we miss her very much.

We wish it didn't have to be this way. We wish she could still be with us. But we know it is this way. And that's hard.

2

Why does God allow suffering and death?

~

People have been asking that since people were first created. And no one has come up with an answer that satisfies everyone.

God is all-loving, but he lets us make choices. He never forces us to choose what is good, to choose what is best for us and everyone else around us.

Any one of us can choose what is bad. We can choose to hurt others and ourselves. We can choose to turn away from God. We call that sin. And we live in a world where a lot of people choose what is bad and then there are a lot of bad consequences.

There's a story in the first book of the Bible that says the first man and woman chose what is bad. God told them that from then on there would be suffering and there would be death. Those things came from what they chose.

But there was a person who never chose what is bad. Never did anything wrong. Never sinned. His story is in the second part of the Bible.

That was Jesus, God's Son. Even though he never did anything wrong, he suffered and he died. And because he did, suffering and death isn't the end for us. We can choose eternal joy and eternal life. All of us will suffer here on earth. All of us will die.

But all of us can live happily ever after with God, with Jesus, and with all our loved ones who have already died and gone to heaven.

3
Why didn't I get a chance to say good-bye?

~

Death can come suddenly and unexpectedly and then we don't get a chance to see our loved one just one last time. And that's very hard, especially if the last time we saw him we were in a rush or we were mad at him or he was mad at us.

Even when somebody is sick for a long time and we all know he's going to die, he may die before we get a chance to see him one last time.

When that happens — either way — it can help to remember that he knew we loved him and we know he loved us. We wish we had had a few final words and one last hug, but we have to make do with unspoken good-byes. One was in his heart then, just as one is in our hearts — in your heart — now.

4
Why didn't prayers make him all better?

~

God always answers our prayers. Sometimes the answer is "yes" and sometimes it's "no."

It can be very hard when the answer is no. That's when we need faith. That means we believe God is taking care of him, and of us, even when it feels like he isn't.

5
Is she really never coming back?

~

At the end of time but not in our lifetimes. That's one reason death is so hard for the people who get left behind. We can't imagine spending the rest of our lives without hearing her voice or touching her hand. Without her telling us a story or going for a walk with us.

Right now you can't imagine the rest of your life without her. Later on, not right away, you won't hurt so much when you think about her. You'll find it's easier to remember how wonderful it was that you two had some time together, even though you may always wish it had lasted longer.

6

Someone said, "She just went to sleep." Why doesn't she wake up?

~

People say that sometimes, because it hurts too much to say she died. Or they might say she "passed away" or she "passed."

But being dead isn't like being asleep. Someone who's dead doesn't wake up because her body isn't working anymore. She might look like she's only sleeping, but her soul — the part of her that will never die — has left her body. It has gone to see God.

7

Someone said, "God took her." Why would God be so mean?

~

God isn't mean, but it can feel that way when someone we love dies. It can be hard to remember that all of us were made to spend just a little time on earth and then all eternity — forever — with God and our loved ones in heaven.

People say that "God took her" or "God called her home" to help remind themselves that even though she's gone from here, she's where she's supposed to be. Where all of us are supposed to be someday.

8

Someone said, "God wanted her." Doesn't he know I want her, too?

~

We all want her. She didn't die because God wanted her more than we wanted her. That's an expression some people use when they're feeling sad about the death of a loved one. It helps some people feel a little better.

9

If I'm really good, will God bring her back?

~

It would be great if God would bring her back if we all agreed to be good. But that doesn't happen. You may wish you could make a deal with God. You agree to do something really hard and he agrees to bring her back to life.

A lot of people have that feeling when someone they love has died. A lot of people wish that's the way it could be. But that's not the way it is when someone dies.

You wish you could do something to change it, but you can't. But that doesn't mean you can't do anything. What you can do — what each of us can do — is help the other people around us who are hurting, too. We can help one another. That doesn't bring her back, but it can make it a little easier during this really hard time when we're first missing her.

10
Why do some babies die?

~

A baby might die because she was born with a health problem or because she got sick. Maybe she was hurt in an accident or someone hurt her. And sometimes a baby dies and no one knows the reason why. The doctors and the scientists can't say why the baby died.

Even when we know what caused a baby's death, we still don't know why that particular baby died. Why is her life over and another baby's life just beginning? We don't have an answer for that.

The answer to your very good question is we don't have an answer. And all of us — young and old — wish we did.

11
Why did he kill himself?

~

We might be able to guess why he chose suicide, why he thought he had to take his own life, but we don't really know.

Maybe because his problems seemed so big he didn't see any way out. Maybe because his brain wasn't working right and he thought that was the right thing to do or the only way to stop hurting.

It's extra hard for those of us who loved him because we wonder if we could have done something more — or something different — to help him solve his problems or help him get the right medicine or therapy.

Only God knows what happened, but we know God loves him. We believe he's in God's hands now and God will take care of him.

12
Why was she killed?

It just doesn't make sense when someone we love is taken from us because of an accident or an act of violence. We ask ourselves why one thing wasn't different, to make it all different.

Why didn't she go home a different way? Why was she at that place at that time?

Sometimes people are killed accidentally and it's nobody's fault. It's a bad thing that just happened. And sometimes someone is responsible. It's his fault that she died.

When that's the way it is, it's hard not to be angry at the person who took the life of the one we love. Of course we are very angry. And it may take time for that anger to leave us. It doesn't mean we're bad because we're angry, but just because we're angry doesn't mean we can do bad things.

If you can talk about being angry, and you can show that you're angry in ways that don't hurt you or anybody else, over time that anger won't feel so big inside you. Over time it will get smaller, but it may never disappear.

It may always be inside you and that can be a good thing. It can be that little bit of anger that helps you be a better person, helps you appreciate life more, helps you protect it.

13
Why would someone want to kill him?

~

Sometimes people kill other people without meaning to. They make a mistake or they do something wrong — like playing around with a gun or driving after they've been drinking alcohol — and they cause a death. They don't want to kill anybody. They don't want to kill someone we love. But they do.

And sometimes people do mean to kill someone else. Someone in particular. They don't like that person. Or they're afraid of that person. Or they don't like what that person has done.

And sometimes people kill someone else, but they don't even know that person. They kill a man because he looks like he has money. They kill a woman because they want to hurt her. They kill a stranger just because of where that person is, or what that person does, or how that person looks.

No matter how — or why — somebody kills someone you love, it feels like that person killed a little piece of you, too. And, in a way, that person did. He or she killed the earthly relationship that you two shared. That person killed the way you shared that special bond by killing your loved one.

Of course we want to know why someone killed the person we love. But there's never a good answer. Never one that makes the hurting suddenly go away.

III

What Comes Next

14
Where is she now?
What comes
after death?

~

Each of us — including you — is made up of a body and a soul. We can see our bodies. We can feel them. But we can't see our souls. We can't feel them. When we die, our souls leave our bodies. Our bodies stay here and our souls go to God.

Her body is here. We can still see it. But her soul has gone. Now it can see God face to face or it's still getting ready to see God face to face. Her soul must be pretty excited and happy. She gets to see the One who created her!

15
What's a soul?

~

A soul is the spiritual part of each us. Each soul is one of a kind, created by God when a person's body is created. It keeps going, it stays alive, even after the body stops living.

At the end of time, each dead body will get its soul back, each human will be fully alive again, and will stay that way forever.

16
Is he an angel now?

~

No. God made angels and he made people, but they're two different kinds of creations. Angels don't have bodies. They're only spiritual beings. People have bodies and souls. When a body dies, the soul can go to heaven and be with God and with the angels and the souls of other people who have died.

17
Is she a ghost now?
~

No, ghosts are make-believe. They're in stories that people make up just for fun.

Now her body is here, but it doesn't have life in it anymore. And her soul has gone to be with God.

Sometimes there are stories or television shows or movies about the ghosts of people who have died, but those stories are just pretend.

18
Is she a saint now?

～

She could be. The Church says every soul in heaven is a saint. Some of them have been "canonized" — that means recognized and honored by the Church in a special way. Those are the saints we name our parishes and schools for.

But every soul in heaven is a saint. So when her soul is ready to see God, and she's in heaven, then she's a saint, too.

Her feast day will be November 1, All Saints' Day.

19
What is heaven like?

Heaven is our final, true home. It's better than anything you can imagine. You can pray to God on earth, but in heaven you'll get to see him.

God created heaven and he created you to be there with him. All of us are on a journey through this world on our way to heaven. Our last stop here is death. That's the gate, or the way, to a new and wonderful life that will never end.

Heaven is perfect. It's not somewhere up in the clouds. It's being with God. In heaven, someday, all of us can be happy together forever. In heaven there is no sickness or pain or death. There's only joy.

20
Do pets go to heaven?

Some people love animals so much they can't imagine a happy place without them. We know heaven is the happiest place ever and we know God wants us to be happy so we just have to leave it up to him.

So do pets go to heaven? We can't say yes, for sure. And we can't no, for sure. What we can say is God will take care of it and he knows we won't be disappointed.

21
Who goes to hell?
What is it like?

~

The souls of the people who completely say "no" to God and want nothing to do with God choose hell. More than a place, hell is a condition. It's a very sad way for some people to be, because they are the ones who have rejected God, the source of life and joy.

22
What is purgatory?

Purgatory is how the souls who aren't ready to see God take the time to get ready. We can pray for the souls in purgatory, asking God to help them get ready to see him. Every soul getting ready in purgatory will someday go to heaven.

23
What is limbo?

A long time ago people weren't sure what happened to a baby who died before he could be baptized. They didn't know how he could get to heaven without being baptized, but they didn't see how God would let a little baby be in hell.

So they thought maybe there was a place called "limbo." They said it was a place just like heaven except God wasn't there.

Now the Church says even those who aren't formally baptized can go to heaven. We think if a baby had a choice, if a baby could pick, he would pick being with God.

24
Why do we pray for her?

~

We pray that, as soon as possible, her soul is ready to go see God. We ask God to forgive her for the mistakes she made, for the sins she committed, and welcome her into his wonderful kingdom. Knowing that our prayers can help her may help us feel better and keep us connected to her.

25
Why do we pray to her?

Praying is talking. When we pray to God, we're talking to him. When we pray to a loved one who has died, we're doing the same thing.

Just like we asked for her help when she was alive, we ask for it now even though she has died. We believe she can pray for us. She can ask God to help us.

26
Did our love die, too?

No! When someone we love dies, we can still love him and he can still love us!

We are all part of what's called the "communion of saints." That's the angels and souls in heaven. The souls in purgatory. And those of us here on earth. We can all pray for one another. We can all love each other.

27
Can he see me?
~

We don't know if he sees you like he did when he was alive, but he still loves you very much and wants nothing but the best for you.

28
Is God mad at her because she didn't go to church?

~

Oh, no. God loves her. He always loved her and he always will, just like he loves you and always will. There's nothing you can ever do — nothing she could ever do — to stop God's love.

God wants her to be happy in heaven with him forever. That's what he wants for you, too.

Going to church is a way to help us know God better and love God better. It helps us get home to him.

IV

A Child's Own Reactions

29
Is this my fault?

~

When someone we love dies, we feel so terrible it's easy to start asking ourselves if we did something wrong that helped cause that death.

We so want things to be different that we think maybe if we had done something differently, this wouldn't have happened.

It isn't your fault. Don't blame yourself. I'll say it again: It isn't your fault.

30
Did he die because I was bad?

~

That's another way of asking, "Is this my fault?" The answer is no. It isn't your fault. He didn't die because of something you did do or because of something you didn't do.

31
Did he die because he was bad?

~

No. Everyone dies, good people and bad people. Jesus died. Mary died. And they were the best people ever.

32
Will I always feel this awful?

~

No. But it may take a while before you start feeling better. And then you may feel OK for a few days or weeks or even months, and then feel really sad all over again.

That's normal. You are grieving and it takes time to work through grief.

33
What is grief?

~

Grief is the horrible way we feel — which affects both our bodies and our minds — when we lose someone, or something, that was irreplaceable.

Sometimes the loss is so big, the hole we feel in our hearts and in our lives is so huge, we have trouble eating or sleeping, or even thinking.

People may grieve — have grief or, as we say, suffer with grief — for a long time after a loved one dies. If you feel that way, it's very normal. It may help you to talk about how you feel. It may help to remember him in a special way. It may help to get busy sometimes doing something you used to enjoy doing.

Over time, the grief isn't so intense, it isn't so strong. It will go down a notch or two and then, you'll start to feel like your old self. You'll still be sad when you think about him, but it won't be a sadness so deep and so powerful you almost feel paralyzed, you almost feel like you can't even move.

It may not seem possible right now, but, with time, things are going to be OK.

34
Will I ever be happy again?

Yes. It may take time, but you'll be happy again. You'll laugh and you'll want to go play. You aren't going to feel so sad forever.

35
Why can't I stop thinking about her?

~

It's hard to not think about something that's causing us pain. If we twist an ankle, all we seem to think about is our ankle. How much it hurts. And how much we use it to get around.

It's kind of the same thing when someone we love dies. It hurts. You don't have to be told that. You know how much it hurts.

When someone we loves dies, we think about her. We remember what she's meant to us. We remember the times we spent together. And then we can't help but think about — can't help but imagine — the times that she won't be around. We imagine going on without her. And, in a way, we're limping. It hurts to keep going, but we know we have to keep going.

36
What if I forget him?

Each one of us has special memories of him. You may remember things that I don't remember. I may remember things that you don't remember. That's what's so wonderful about sharing memories, about telling favorite stories.

We can remind one another about this wonderful person we loved so much. The one we still love and who still loves us.

If your memory of him seems to be fading sometime, or if you have a question about him, you ask me. And I'll tell you a story.

And if my memory gets a little hazy, if I have a question about him that you can answer or I want to hear a story, I'll ask you.

We'll remember together.

37

Am I bad because I'm kind of mad at her for leaving? Are you mad at her, too?

~

I'm not surprised you feel mad. At times I feel mad, too. I want her to still be here with us. I want that so badly I start to blame her for leaving. As if it were her fault she died.

But everybody is going to die. And sometimes it's nobody's fault.

38

Am I bad because I kind of feel glad he's dead?

~

No, that doesn't mean you're bad. Sometimes when a person dies, we do feel glad even while we're feeling sad. It could be we're glad that he's out of pain now. He had so many medical problems that just staying alive was hard for him. And now he has nothing but happiness.

And sometimes we feel a little glad about a death because that person hurt us or hurt someone we love. And now we know he's not going to hurt anyone anymore.

39

Why am I afraid to be alone or go to sleep?

~

Death is frightening. It scares grown-ups, so you shouldn't be surprised it scares someone your age.

What do we like when we're scared? We like to be around other people. We feel safer then. We like to be alert — to stay on guard. And that means not falling asleep.

What you're describing is something lots of us have: very normal reactions. With time, it will feel OK to be alone. You may even prefer it. And it won't seem scary to go to sleep.

40
Why can't I stop crying?

After a while, you won't cry as often as you do now. Right now, if you feel like crying, then go ahead and cry. Over time, the pain — that whole jumble of emotions you feel — will start to ease up a little bit. Then there won't be as many tears.

41
Why can't I sleep?

When someone you love dies, your emotions get all stirred up. You might feel sad and scared and confused and mad all at the same time. Your body can hurt and your mind seems to be going a million miles an hour — or not moving at all.

All that can make it hard to sleep. But even if you can't fall asleep, it can help if you rest. If you lie down and take a little break. After the death of somebody you love, you may want to keep a light on in the bedroom, even if you're a big kid. Or keep the door open. Or let the radio play some soft music. Those are fine if they help you rest.

Even if you're a big kid and haven't taken naps for a long time, maybe resting in the middle of the day will help you feel a little better.

42
Why am I so tired?

~

You may be so tired because it's hard to get a good night's sleep. And there's so much going on right now, it's hard to be calm. Hard to relax.

And all those emotions inside you take energy. Grieving makes you tired. More than tired. Exhausted. That means really, really tired.

Our lives will start to settle down in a while. Then it will be easier to get some sleep. Easier to start feeling more rested.

43
Why does my stomach hurt?

~

It's all those emotions. All those feelings churning around inside you, like clothes in a washing machine.

If we pay attention to what you eat and we make sure you get some rest, even if you can't sleep, you'll probably start to feel better. And if you get some exercise, too. If you get the chance to ride your bike or shoot some hoops.

44

Am I bad because for a little while I forgot she was dead?

~

No, we can't think about that all the time. As time goes by and we start to feel a little better, we begin to think about other things, too. And that's good. We begin to feel like doing some of the fun things we used to do. And that's good, too.

We know she wants us to think about a lot of things. To do other things. To have fun.

45
I thought I saw her today. Did I?

~

No, but it's easy to make that mistake. When someone is on our mind a lot, another person may look like her. Maybe it was the way that stranger walked or the way she stood. Maybe it was her hair-style or her clothes.

What happened to you isn't unusual. After a loved one dies, and we see someone who reminds us of her, just for an instant we can think it *is* her.

46
Will I ever see him again?

~

We wish we could see him right now. You know we can't. But we will see him again. You will see him again. When it's time for you to go to heaven. As you get older, you'll have more and more loved ones in heaven and on earth. We stay with the ones on earth until God calls us to be with the ones in heaven.

47
Are you going to die?

~

Someday. Dying is the only way we get to go to heaven. That's where we all belong. But that doesn't mean I want to die. And it certainly doesn't mean I'm going to die soon. We leave the when and the how up to God.

48
Am I going to die?

Someday, but we pray that doesn't happen for a long, long time. But someday, after we're all dead, we'll be together in heaven forever. We'll live forever there.

49
Why am I dying?

Sometimes a young person is sick or a part of his body doesn't work right. Then he doesn't live as long as most people do.

There's not a good reason for why that has happened to you and not to someone else. We just don't understand why it's so. We don't want it to be that way. But we know we can't change it.

Sometimes all the love and all the prayers in the world can't change something. I wish with all my heart they could. I wish you and I could change places. I wish I could give you my health and my long life, and I could take your sickness and your short life.

While you're still here, I will love you and pray for you every day. Later, when you're in heaven, we can still love each other. And when you're in heaven, I want you to please pray for me. You say lots of prayers for me.

50
Why are you dying?

~

I don't know why some people die at my age and some people live to be very old.

I do know I will always love you. Always.

I do know I will always pray for you. Always.

I do know God loves both of us. And someday you and I can be in heaven together. For always.

51

Can I talk to him?
Does he hear me?
Will he talk to me?

~

Yes, you can talk to him. You can do it out loud or just in your head. He'll hear you. You can ask him to say prayers for you. You can still ask for his help. He would certainly want to keep helping you.

(This talking to one another, praying for one another, among the people on earth, the souls in purgatory, and the souls in heaven is known as the "communion of saints.")

He won't talk to you like he used to. Not like a voice you can hear out loud. But sometimes it will seem as if he's talking to you. In your head. You may remember him saying one of his favorite expressions or his words of advice. You may remember a story about him and, in your head, hear what he said then. You may imagine what he would say or how he would react when you tell him something now.

Maybe you want to pick a particular time to talk to him. Mass can be a good time to do that. He is with Jesus — with God — all the time now and Jesus comes to us in a special way in Holy Communion. You can talk to him and to Jesus in a special way at Mass.

52

How can we have Christmas without her?

It doesn't seem possible, does it? But we know she would want us to have a good Christmas. She would want us to appreciate one another more, now that we have to celebrate the day without her.

You may feel sad all over again on Christmas. You may miss her a lot on that day. The same with your birthday. And her birthday. And you may feel extra sad again on the anniversary of her death.

A lot of people feel that way on those days.

We'll have Christmas by being sad together and by being happy together. We'll have Christmas by being together. It will be different from the other Christmases we had, but it can still be a good one.

53

Why do I still think he's not dead?

The death of a loved one is a hard thing to accept, a hard thing to believe. We don't want it to be true. And we wish it weren't.

It can be so overwhelming that it just doesn't seem real.

We think maybe we're dreaming. We hope we're dreaming because then we can wake up and he'll still be alive.

It may take you some time to accept the fact that he's dead. Some time before you really believe he's dead. That's normal. A lot of us feel that way.

V
Funerals
and
Cemeteries

54
What is a "funeral home"?
~

That's the place where a body is taken to get it ready for the funeral and the burial. The funeral-home workers dress the body in his good clothes and put him in a coffin.

55
How does the funeral home get his good clothes?

~

The family members pick out something nice from the person's closet and bring it to the home.

56
Why is it called a funeral "home"?

~

It used to be common that large homes were used for this business. It's a name that just stuck. Another traditional name is "funeral parlor."

57
What is a "mortician"?

That's another name for the funeral-home worker. Sometimes he or she is called an "undertaker." That's the person who helps get the body ready for the funeral and for burial and helps get the body moved from the funeral home to the church to the cemetery.

58
What is "embalming"?

That's a way bodies are prepared for burial. It's a custom now in many countries.

59
What's the difference between a casket and a coffin?

They mean the same thing. It's the special box used to carry a body.

It has handles on both sides so it can be carried. And it can be set on a special stand with wheels so it can be moved around more easily.

60
What does "cremation" mean?
~

Sometimes a body is buried or put into a tomb and sometimes it's cremated. Cremation means burning a body into ashes. It doesn't hurt because after a body has died, it can't feel anything.

(For a time the Catholic Church didn't allow cremation, but now it does.)

61
How is a body cremated?

≈

The body is taken to the crematory. That can be at the funeral home. It's placed in a "retort" — a big container. Then natural gas is used — like a furnace — to burn the body until there is nothing left but ashes.

The ashes are put into an urn — a special small box that might look like a metal vase — and that's taken to the cemetery. Sometimes the urn is buried and sometimes it's placed in a mausoleum, a building for coffins and urns.

Some people take the ashes to a place the person liked and "spread" his ashes there. (The Catholic Church does not want people to do this. It says a body — whole or cremated — should be in a cemetery.)

62
What is a "viewing"?

That's a time set aside for friends to come to the funeral home and pay their respects to the person who has died and to offer their sympathy to the person's family. It might be for a few hours one evening or it could be over several days.

63
What is a "vigil"?

A vigil is a time of prayer in the funeral home or in the church. Friends and family gather before the funeral. Sometimes the night before. Sometimes right before.

In the past, it was customary to say a rosary during the vigil. That's still done sometimes. Other times it's different prayers or readings from the Bible.

64
What is a "wake"?

Originally that was like a viewing. When people lived in big homes, the body might be taken there and friends and neighbors would come by to pay their respects and offer sympathy to the family.

When the parish priest showed up, prayers were said for the person who died. Often that prayer was the rosary.

Food and drink were served to visitors.

This is a custom that split into two traditions. One is the vigil. The other — sometimes still called a "wake" — is a gathering (without the body) to celebrate that person's life and to console one another.

65
What are "mourners"?
~

They are the family and friends of the person who died. To "mourn" means to be very sad.

66
What is a "survivor"?

That's the word that's used for the dead person's relatives who are still alive. If a man dies and his wife is still alive, we say, "He is 'survived' by her."

67
What is an "obituary"?

That's a notice in the newspaper about the person who died. Usually, it also has information about the services that are going to be held.

68
Who writes what's said in the obituary?

~

A family member may write what's in the newspaper with some help from the people at the funeral home. Or the people at the funeral home may write it for the family after the family gives them information about the person who died.

An obituary usually includes when and where the person was born. When and where he died. Where he lived and some of the jobs he had or what kind of work he did. Who the members of his immediate family are. When and where his services are going to be held and when and where he's going to be buried. And what charity he would have liked, or his family would like, donations to be made in his memory. That means in his name, in honor of him.

69

Why did her obituary say "and grandchildren" instead of giving my name like it gave yours?

~

Obituaries come in different styles and they can be written in different ways. They also have different costs. Longer ones cost more money.

The family thought this was the best one for her. It certainly doesn't mean that you aren't important. We all know you loved her and she loved you.

70
What happens at the funeral?

~

The funeral director brings the body to the church and the pallbearers carry it inside. The coffin is in the back of the church and the family is nearby to greet people who are coming to the service. They stop by to see the body, to offer sympathy to the family, and to sign the guest book.

If the coffin has been open, the funeral director closes it when it's time to begin the funeral. Then the priest gathers the family around the coffin and says some prayers. During the funeral the coffin is sprinkled with holy water and incensed with smoke.

The family walks up to the front of the church as the coffin is wheeled up front. Father says a Mass and during it he says special prayers for the person who has died and for the family and friends of the dead person.

After Mass, the body is wheeled to the back of the church and the pallbearers carry it back to the hearse, the special car for the coffin.

71
Do I have to do something at the funeral?

~

There aren't any rules about that. In some families, people like to bring up the gifts during the Mass or read one of the readings or help with Holy Communion. If the family decides we would like to divide up some jobs and you're asked if you would like to help with one, you can say yes or no. Either way is fine.

72
What do people wear to funerals?
~

People wear their best clothes as a sign of respect for the person who has died.

73
Why do we use special cars?

~

We need a car big enough to hold the coffin when we take Grandpa from the funeral home to the church and from the church to the cemetery. This special car is called a hearse.

Grandma has asked that all her children — your aunts and uncles and me — go together in the same car with her and so we'll use a special car for that, too.

74
Will I get to ride in a special car?
~

☐ Yes.
☐ No. You'll be riding with _____.

75
Will I ride in the same car with you?
~

Sometimes family members ride in different cars because they need to be with different people. For example, a grown-up man may ride with his father instead of with his wife and children because the grandpa needs extra love and support right then.

I'll let you know who's riding in which car as soon it's been decided. And if you don't like your assignment, you let me know. Maybe I can change it and maybe I can't. Maybe on that day, to help out everybody, you'll have to settle for something that wasn't your first choice.

If that's the case, it's important you be very polite about it. You do it without any complaining. That's a way you can be a big help to the family.

76
Why can't I go to the funeral?
~

That's a decision we made. It's very hard to go to a funeral, especially when you're young. We think it's best if you don't go and, instead, you remember him the way he was when he was alive.

But even so, both of us can say prayers together for him here.

77
Is it OK to be afraid of her body?
~

Of course it is. Part of the reason it seems scary is because her body kind of looks like her and it kind of doesn't. And it's scary because there are so many stories about dead people. We know those stories are just pretend, that they're just made up, but they can still scare us. It could be you can't help thinking about some of those stories when you look at her.

It's all right to be afraid, but you don't have to be afraid. You're safe. We're safe.

78
Why didn't he look like himself in the coffin?

Some people look the same and some don't. There are many reasons for this. Sometimes you've only seen that person with his glasses on, and he isn't wearing them in the coffin. Sometimes you've never seen him with his eyes shut, never seen him napping or sleeping. Sometimes you've never seen him all dressed up in his best clothes.

Sometimes you've never seen him without a big smile on his face or a twinkle in his eye. Sometimes you've never seen him be still. He was always, go, go, go! Or you've never seen him when he wasn't laughing or telling a story.

Then, too, when a body dies, the heart doesn't pump blood through it anymore. And it's the oxygen in the blood that gives skin its color and its life. After death, a body's muscles don't work anymore. Muscles help give a face the shape it has. When the muscles don't work anymore, parts of the face can sag.

At the funeral home, the mortician may put makeup on the face — even a man's face — to help it look more lifelike. Sometimes that helps and sometimes it doesn't.

If you don't like the way he looked in the coffin, it can help to think back instead on a happy time with him and remember him that way. At home, you can put out a favorite picture of him.

79
Why couldn't I see his legs?

~

The lid of the coffin is in two parts. The top half was open, but the bottom half was closed.

80
Why was the coffin kept closed?

~

Sometimes the person who is dying tells people that at her funeral, she wants the casket kept closed. She would prefer her family and friends remember her the way she was when she was alive and well, not the way she looks after she has died.

And sometimes the family makes that decision.

If the coffin is closed at a service, it's because the person who died wanted it that way or the family has asked that it be that way.

81
Is the coffin locked?
~

Some coffins have locks. Those ones are sealed shut. Some just have latches. The latch or lock makes it so the lid doesn't come open by accident as it goes from the funeral home to the church and from the church to the cemetery.

One way we honor a deceased person is by treating his body with respect. It would be disrespectful if the top suddenly popped open. It would also be very hard on the family and friends.

The coffin isn't shut tight so the dead person can't get out. A dead person can't move. And it isn't so no one will break in — like locking the front door of our house. It doesn't have a special key that will only open that one coffin.

82
What's a "pallbearer"?

A pallbearer is a person chosen to help carry the coffin. The "pall" is the cloth put over the coffin for the funeral Mass. It's a symbol of the white garment worn at baptism. To "bear" something can mean to carry it. The family chooses the pallbearers. It's an honor to be chosen.

83

Why does the priest use holy water and incense?

The water is a reminder of the water used at baptism. And the incense — the sweet-smelling smoke — shows respect for the body and symbolizes our prayers going up to heaven.

84

What's the difference between a funeral and a memorial?

~

In the Catholic Church, a funeral is a Mass of Christian Burial. The body is present for that. A memorial Mass is a service in the church without the body.

Other religions have different customs. Sometimes a funeral or service is held in a church. Sometimes in a funeral home or cemetery chapel or at the grave. Sometimes a memorial service is held at someone's house or in a park. Sometimes there's only a reception or party. Sometimes there's no ceremony or service or celebration.

85
Why didn't we have a funeral for him?
~

Not everyone has a funeral or memorial service. Not everyone is buried in a cemetery.

It could be that the person who died had told other people what he wanted. And so they do that. Or the family may decide. They try to choose what is right for their loved one and right for the family.

86
Will there be a flag on the coffin?

Some people want to have a flag on the coffin, especially if the dead person has been in military service. If there is, the flag is taken off and the pall put on before the coffin is wheeled up the aisle for the beginning of the funeral.

87
Will there be someone playing the bugle or shooting guns at the cemetery?

∾

Those are military traditions, too. Some graveside ceremonies have them and some don't.

88
Why do some people send flowers?

~

That's a custom. It's a traditional way for people to show they cared about the person who has died and they care about the family and friends left behind.

Sometimes instead of flowers, or in addition to flowers, people make a donation to the dead person's favorite charity or the family's favorite charity. That's another way of showing they care.

89
Why are people buried?

~

That's been the custom for a long, long time. Some countries used cremation, but many others used burial. In either case, part of the reason was health. If the body had been sick with a disease someone else might catch, it was better to keep it away from other people.

And, with burial, part of it was a way of showing respect for the person. They put the body in a special place and then could come back to that place and remember him.

That's what cemeteries — or graveyards — are. Special places where we can come back and remember our loved ones.

90
Who digs the hole?

Sometimes a person has already bought a "plot" — a little piece of land in the cemetery. Other times, the family buys it after a loved one has died. The family or funeral home lets the cemetery workers know there is a body that needs to be buried and the cemetery workers use a backhoe — a kind of tractor — to dig a hole that is six or seven feet deep.

They put a concrete liner inside the hole and then the casket goes into the liner. The cemetery workers are the ones who fill up the hole after the family and friends leave and they put the grass back on top. They make sure the cemetery looks nice all the time.

91
What if a body wakes up after it's buried?

~

That's a scary thought. That's probably why it's such a popular scene in a movie or a book. But that doesn't really happen.

A body that has died doesn't wake up that way. We don't know how everyone's body will "wake up," will come back to life, at the end of time when Jesus comes again. We'll find out then.

92
What's a "headstone"?

A headstone or tombstone is the marker that's used at the cemetery. It could be very simple or very fancy. Often it's made from stone called marble and granite, and the person's name and her dates of birth and death are carved into it.

That is a job some people have. They make the markers and put the writing on them. Usually, the family decides what the headstone will look like and what the writing will say.

93
What does "rest in peace" mean?
~

That's a phrase that goes back a long, long time. A lot of prayers used to be said in Latin and then it was "requiescat in pace," which means "rest in peace." Sometimes you see the initials R.I.P. That's what those letters stand for.

When we pray that someone soul's will rest in peace we mean it will be with God. It's kind of like relaxing, taking it easy, after a hard day at school. Or on a Saturday after a tough week.

After all that happens during a lifetime, a soul can finally rest.

94
What happens right after the funeral?

People who are going to the cemetery get into their cars and they turn on their headlights. Police officers on motorcycles or in police cars help direct traffic as the cars follow the hearse to the cemetery. Cars have their lights on to show they are part of the funeral procession. Other cars stop or pull over to let the procession go by. The procession doesn't have to stop at stop signs or traffic lights.

At the cemetery, the pallbearers carry the coffin to the grave. The priest says a few more prayers there. Sometimes everyone leaves before the coffin is lowered into the grave and sometimes people stay for that.

Sturdy straps are used to gently lower the coffin into the ground.

95
Why do we have a big lunch after the funeral?

~

There's an easy answer. People come to a funeral and then go to a ceremony at the grave and, after all that, they're hungry!

Then, too, the family members are the hosts. They welcome the guests and thank them for coming. Just like when company comes at home, it's nice to be able to offer them something to eat and to drink.

Often members of a parish or friends will help with the meal. They may supply most of the food and help with serving. That's because family members are so busy with all the things it takes to get ready for the funeral, and are so sad and so tired after the death of their loved one, they don't have the time or the energy to do it.

Another reason is they may not have the time and energy to fix food even for themselves and they need to eat, even if they don't feel much like eating.

But there's another big reason for the meal, too. It gives friends and family members a chance to talk to one another. They tell stories about their loved one who has died and they comfort one another. Family members get the chance to thank the other people who came to their loved one's funeral.

96

Why were some people laughing after the vigil and after the funeral? Wasn't that rude?

~

No, they weren't being rude. They weren't being disrespectful. Telling happy stories about the person who has died and remembering happy times with him is one way we all get through such hard times.

After a loved one dies, we cry together, we pray together, and we laugh together. Tears and prayers and laughter. We need all three right then.

97

What am I supposed to do with the memorial card?

~

It's a custom to hand out holy cards or memorial cards at a funeral. A card might have an image of Jesus or a saint or it might have a photograph of the loved one who has died. It usually includes the dates when she was born and when she died. And it often has that person's favorite verses from the Bible or a quote from a poem or reading she liked.

You can put the memorial card on display in your room if you like, or you can save it in a book or drawer. We can save ours together, if you like. We can put your name on yours and when you want it, you can have it.

98

Why do we go back and visit her grave?

~

After a loved one dies, it can be very hard to say just one good-bye. Sometimes it takes a lot of them. That's one reason we go to the cemetery.

We go there to pray for her. We ask God to welcome her into heaven. To forgive her for the mistakes she made while she was alive — and we all make mistakes — and to let her soul be with him and with the angels and the others saints.

We go there to remember her. Our visiting the cemetery is a sign that we loved her very much. It's a way of saying she was an important part of our lives, and even though she is dead now, we love her still. And we always will.

And we go there to say a prayer to her. To talk to her. Sometimes out loud. Sometimes in our hearts. Asking her to remember us in her prayers. To continue to help us now just as she did when she was alive.

VI

Dealing with Others

99
Why is Daddy (Mommy) so mad?
~

When someone we love dies, we might feel mad that he's left us. Or we might feel mad that someone, or some illness, took him from us.

You know that when you're mad at a friend, it's hard not to seem mad at everyone that's around you right then, too.

That can be the way it is after a loved one dies. We might be mad at ourselves, or mad at the one who died, or even mad at God. Other people can see our anger and they think we're mad at them, even though they didn't do anything wrong.

And sometimes we get mad when we don't get enough rest. We get impatient with other people. If we don't get enough sleep, or we don't get our nap, other people just bother us more than if we're rested.

It can be hard to get enough sleep after a loved one dies. There's so much to do and there are so many emotions — so many feelings — running around inside us.

100
Why didn't my cousins cry?

~

Everyone may react a little differently to the death of a loved one because everyone had a relationship that was different than anyone else's. And everyone has his or her own personality — way of reacting and way of doing things.

Some people cry more easily in public than others do. Some people would rather cry only when they're by themselves. Some people don't cry much at all or don't cry at all. Some people cry for a while and then stop for a while.

Some want to be alone and be quiet. Some want to be with others and talk.

It doesn't mean one person is sadder than the other. Or one person doesn't really care that the person has died.

You get to cry when you want to cry. And you get to stop when it feels like it's time to stop. No one is going to make you cry or make you stop crying. Just like no one can force you to feel sadder than you already feel. Or force you to stop feeling sad.

101
What do I say when people say they're sorry?

~

Just say "Thank you." If you want to say more, you can. But if you don't want to, you don't have to.

102
What do I say when people ask me how I'm doing?
~

That can depend on who asks you and how they ask you.

If somebody is saying "how are you?" as a way of just saying "hello," you can answer "OK" or "All right" or "Fine." You don't need to try to explain how you're really doing.

If it's somebody who really wants to know how you're doing, you can give a short answer or a long answer. It's up to you. You can say "OK" or "All right" or "Fine." Or you can talk more about how you really are doing. Whichever way you want.

103

Why do my friends act as if nothing has happened?

~

They may not know what to say to you. And it isn't just children who can have a hard time knowing what to say, it's grown-ups, too.

Some people think there are some "magic words" that will make everything all better for you. But they don't know what those words are and so they don't say anything. Now you know there are no magic words. It just takes time for the hurting to start to go away.

Some people are afraid they'll say the "wrong" thing and make you feel sadder. And so they keep silent, too.

It could be your friends and the kids on the team and in your class have never had a loved one die. They don't know what it's like for you. They just don't know what a big deal it is and how you think about it a lot.

VII

On
Dying

104
Why couldn't I see her in the hospital?

~

Sometimes those who work in a hospital restrict who's allowed to visit and they prefer if young people stay in a waiting room rather than going into a patient's room. And sometimes there are certain sections of the hospital that allow only a small number of visitors. Sections like the intensive care unit or coronary care unit, where patients have special needs and receive special attention.

Sometimes, too, the parents make that decision. It isn't easy seeing a loved one who is very, very sick. They believe it may be too much for a young child to understand.

And sometimes it's the patient who asks that children wait outside. It could be those patients don't want all the medical equipment to scare their grandchildren. Or they know they don't look very good right then because they have been so sick, and they don't want to frighten their grandchildren. They think it's better if the younger children remember them the way they used to be — up and around. And the way they used to look — in much better health.

105
Who told you he was dead?

It was _____.

Some members of a person's family may be with him when he dies, and they can see he's dead. Or, if the family isn't there when he dies, the medical people or someone else like a sheriff or police officer tells the immediate family. "Immediate family" means the ones most closely related to him, like a mom or dad, a brother or sister, or a son or daughter.

Usually the immediate family then tells the extended family — the other relatives — and the friends. Sometimes a relative or friend then helps out by calling other relatives and friends. That's how people find out he has died and when and where the services for him are going to be held.

And usually there's a notice in the local newspaper that says he has died. That's called an obituary. (See Nos. 67, 68, and 69.)

106
Does it hurt to die?

A disease or an illness can hurt. You know what it's like to have a sore throat or a stomachache. And an accident can hurt. You know what it feels like to stub your toe or scrape your knee.

There can be pain up to the point of death, up until the instant that someone dies. And there can be no pain. It depends on how a person dies. It depends on what killed him.

But there's no reason to think death itself, that moment when someone stopped living, was painful.

Then his soul gets to go see God. And we feel a lot of pain. We hurt because now he's not here anymore. But the pain he felt because of his illness or accident ends.

107
How did they know she was really dead?

~

The medical people — the doctors and nurses — check carefully before they say someone is dead. They don't rely on just what they can see with their own eyes. They have a lot of equipment that helps them make sure if they have any doubt.

There was no mistake. She's really dead.

108
Why did it take so long for her to die?

~

Sometimes death is quick. A heart suddenly stops and the person's life ends. And sometimes death is slow. A disease or illness gradually takes away a person's health.

We don't know why some people have one kind of death and other people have a different kind.

109
What does "pull the plug" mean?

That means take a person off medical machines that are helping his body perform some functions — do some things like breathe. Because the machine is on, some of those functions can keep going even after a person has died or is very near death and is certain to die soon.

We think life is precious and so we want a person to live as long as he can. But we know no one can live forever. The machines are sometimes called "extraordinary measures" and deciding when and how to use them is very serious.

110
What is "euthanasia"?

That means ending a life on purpose before it would stop naturally.

111
What did she die of?

The official cause of death was _____.
That means her body _____.

112
What is a "death certificate"?
~

That's a legal document signed by a doctor saying when and where and how a person died.

113
What is an "autopsy"?

That's an examination of the body after the person has died. It's used to find out the cause of death. There's an autopsy if the doctors don't know why someone died or if that person died while she wasn't under medical care.

114
What was it like when she died?

She was at _____. The people with her were _____.

115
Did she talk about me?

She loved to talk about you. And even when she was too sick or too tired to say much at all, we know you were in her thoughts and prayers.

116
Will her body ever work again?

We believe that at the end of time, Jesus is coming back in a special way. And when he does, all the people who have died will get their bodies back. Just like Jesus rose from the dead — on Easter — everyone else will, too. He was just the first. Someday it will be everyone.

117
What does "organ donor" mean?

~

Our organs are parts of our bodies that do special jobs. Our eyes help us see. Our heart pumps blood. Our lungs fill up with air.

Sometimes when a body dies, some of the organs are still in good shape and they can be used in someone else's body. An organ might make that other person have a better life. Or it may even be what keeps him alive.

To be a "donor" means to give something.

Someone who is an "organ donor" has filled out a legal document that says, "If I die and some of my organs can help others, I want to give them to those people to help them."

So after he is dead, doctors take out the organs that can be used, and other doctors put them into the people who need them.

118

Don't some people almost die and then come back? Why didn't he come back?

~

In some cases a person's heart and breathing may stop for a little while and then with medical help, they start going again. We sometimes say he "died" or "was dead" for that time.

Then, too, there's what we call a "near death experience." It means the person almost died, but he didn't really die. Sometimes people who have almost died have a memory of what that seemed like to them.

But a person who has really died — not "almost" but completely — can't "undie" and come back.

119
Now what happens to her stuff?

~

Some people have a will. That's an official letter that says, "After I die, I want these things to go to these people." The people who make sure the will is followed are the lawyer and the executor. Often a family member or friend has been chosen to be executor.

Some people don't have a will and if that's the case, there are laws that help decide who gets what. And some people make an unofficial list or have told people what they would like to go to whom.

With or without a will, after a loved one dies, sorting through her things and deciding who gets what and what goes where is one of the jobs the survivors have.

Conclusion:
The Good News

Your child may have been taught that the word "Gospel" means "good news," but that had little or no meaning.

Until now.

The good news is that Jesus — a human being and the Son of God — didn't stay dead. He came back to life. And he was only the first.

The good news is that all of us — because of Jesus — will do the same someday.

The good news is that, someday, your child and that special person he or she misses so much right now can spend all eternity together. In heaven, a family reunited, friends rejoined, will celebrate forever at a party — a feast, a banquet — where (to quote Revelation 2:14) God "will wipe every tear" from our eyes. And "death will be no more; mourning and crying and pain will be no more."

No tears. No mourning. No death. Only eternal joy with our loved ones and our God.

That's the good news. That's the best news ever.

Sources

Caring for Your Aging Parent: A Guide for Catholic Families, by Monica and Bill Dodds (Huntington, Ind.: Our Sunday Visitor, 1997).

Catechism of the Catholic Church, Second Edition (Washington, D.C.: United States Catholic Conference, Inc. and Vatican City: Libreria Editrice Vaticana, 1994, 1997).

Catholic Book of the Dead, by Ann Ball (Huntington, Ind.: Our Sunday Visitor, 1995).

Handbook of Prayers, Father James Socias, general editor (Princeton, N.J.: Scepter Publishers, 1995).

On Death and Dying, by Elisabeth Kübler-Ross (New York: The Macmillan Company, 1969).

Prayers

To the Father, Son, and Spirit

Heavenly Father, send your angels and saints to welcome _____ to his (her) new home.

Jesus, take him (her) by the hand and give him (her) a hug for us.

Holy Spirit, be with us now. We miss him (her) very much. Amen.

To the Blessed Mother

Blessed Mother, you know how we feel. You were there when your Son was killed. Watch over _____ and watch over us until that day when we can all be together again. Amen.

A Prayer for Each Other

Lord, thank you for _____. We hurt so much now because we love him (her) so much. Help us help each other during this very hard time. Amen.

Dear God, We Feel Awful

Dear God, we feel awful. We miss _____ and we don't understand why he (she) had to die. No words take away our pain. No explanations satisfy our anger. Right now we just feel bad and mad. Amen.

We Will Always Love

Jesus, we wish things could be different. We wish this was all a bad dream. We wish we had said things and done things differently. Now it seems too late. But the part of _____ that was _____ is still alive. Now he (she) is with you. So we say to you, and to him (her), that we love _____ and always will. Amen.

COME, HOLY SPIRIT

Come, Holy Spirit, sooth our aching hearts.
Come, Holy Spirit, fill our empty hearts.
Come, Holy Spirit, mend our broken hearts.
Come, Holy Spirit.

LORD, WE REMEMBER

Lord, we remember the time _____ made us laugh, and we thank you.

Lord, we remember the time _____ made us feel so special, and we thank you.

Lord, we remember the time _____ helped us when we were hurting, and we thank you.

Lord, we remember the time _____ showed us how much he (she) loves us, and we thank you.

Lord, we remember _____ and we thank you. Amen.

Traditional Prayers

SIGN OF THE CROSS

In the name of the Father, and of the Son, and of the Holy Spirit. Amen.

OUR FATHER

Our Father, who art in heaven, hallowed be thy name. Thy kingdom come; thy will be done on earth as it is in heaven.

Give us this day our daily bread; and forgive us our trespasses as we forgive those who trespass against us; and lead us not into temptation but deliver us from evil. Amen.

HAIL MARY

Hail Mary, full of grace, the Lord is with you; blessed are you among women, and blessed is the fruit of your womb, Jesus.

Holy Mary, Mother of God, pray for us sinners now and at the hour of our death. Amen.

GLORY BE

Glory be to the Father, and to the Son, and to the Holy Spirit.

As it was in the beginning, is now, and ever shall be, world without end. Amen.

ETERNAL REST

Eternal rest grant unto him (her), O Lord.

And let perpetual light shine upon him (her).

May his (her) soul and the souls of the faithful departed, through the mercy of God, rest in peace. Amen.

Into Your Hands, O Lord

Into your hands, O Lord,
we humbly entrust _____.
In this life you embraced him (her)
with your tender love;
deliver him (her) now from every evil
and bid him (her) enter eternal rest.
The old order has passed away;
welcome him (her), then, into paradise,
where there will be no more sorrow,
no weeping or pain,
but the fullness of peace and joy
with your Son and the Holy Spirit
forever and ever. Amen.

Blessed Are Those

Blessed are those who have died in the Lord;
let them rest from their labors,
for their good deeds go with them.

May the Love of God

May the love of God and the peace
of the Lord Jesus Christ
bless and console us
and gently wipe every tear from our eyes:
in the name of the Father,
and of the Son, and of the Holy Spirit. Amen.

To Pray the Rosary

Sign of the Cross

Apostles' Creed

I believe in God, the Father almighty,
creator of heaven and earth.
And in Jesus Christ, his only Son, our Lord,
who was conceived by the Holy Spirit, born of
the Virgin Mary,
suffered under Pontius Pilate, was crucified,
died, and was buried.
He descended into hell; the third day he rose
again from the dead.
He ascended into heaven and sits at the right
hand of God, the Father Almighty;
from thence he shall come to judge the living
and the dead.
I believe in the Holy Spirit, the holy Catholic
Church, the communion of saints,
the forgiveness of sins, the resurrection of the
body, and life everlasting. Amen.

Our Father
Three Hail Marys
Glory Be

Five decades consisting of:
Our Father
Ten Hail Marys
Glory Be

Hail Holy Queen

Hail, Holy Queen, mother of mercy,
our life, our sweetness, and our hope.
To you do we cry,
poor, banished children of Eve.
To you do we send up our sighs,
mourning and weeping in this valley of tears.
Turn then, most gracious advocate,
your eyes of mercy toward us,
and after this our exile
show unto us the blessed fruit of your womb,
   Jesus.
O clement, O loving, O sweet Virgin Mary.
Pray for us, O Holy Mother of God.
That we may be made worthy of the promises
   of Christ.

Let us pray:

O God, whose only begotten Son, by his life, death, and resurrection, has purchased for us the rewards of eternal life, grant, we beseech you, that meditating upon these mysteries of the most holy rosary of the Blessed Virgin Mary, we may imitate what they contain and obtain what they promise, through the same Christ Our Lord. Amen.

ABOUT THE MYSTERIES OF THE ROSARY

While it doesn't have to, traditionally each decade focuses on a particular event in the life of Jesus or Mary.

The Joyful Mysteries are said on Mondays and Thursdays and on the Sundays of Advent.
1. The Annunciation (Luke 1:30-33)
2. The Visitation (Luke 1:50-53)
3. The Nativity (Luke 2:10-11)
4. The Presentation (Luke 2:22-32)
5. The Finding of Jesus in the Temple (Luke 2:48-52)

The Sorrowful Mysteries are said on Tuesdays and Fridays and on the Sundays of Lent.
1. The Agony in the Garden (Matthew 26:38-39)
2. The Scourging at the Pillar (John 19:1)
3. The Crowning of Thorns (Mark 15:16-17)
4. The Carrying of the Cross (John 19:17)
5. The Crucifixion (John 19:28-30)

The Glorious Mysteries are said on Wednesdays and Saturdays and on Sundays outside Advent and Lent.
1. The Resurrection (Mark 16:6-8)
2. The Ascension (Acts 1:10-11)
3. The Descent of the Holy Spirit (Acts 2:1-4)
4. The Assumption (Song of Songs 2:3-6)
5. The Coronation of the Blessed Virgin (Luke 1:51-54)

Index

F

fatigue, 18

fault, 16, 34, 54, 55, 62

flag, 113

flowers, 115

funeral(s), *also* funeral director, funeral home,
80, 81, 82, 83, 87, 88, 89, 94, 96, 97, 98,
99, 102, 104, 107, 108, 109, 111, 112, 113,
117, 121, 122, 123, 124

G

ghost(s), 41

gifts during the Mass, 97

God, 16, 19, 23, 24, 26, 28, 29, 30, 31, 33, 38,
39, 40, 41, 42, 43, 44, 45, 46, 47, 48, 49,
52, 71, 72, 75, 76, 120, 125, 128, 136, 151,
155, 157, 158, 159, 160

good-bye, 19, 25, 125

good news, 151

Gospel, 151

grave, 19, 111, 121, 122, 125

grief, *also* grief minister, 13, 15, 16, 17, 18,
19, 57, 58

guilt, 16

H

happy, 38, 43, 44, 52, 59, 77, 105, 123

headaches, 18

headstone, 119

hearse, 96, 121

heaven, 24, 29, 40, 42, 43, 44, 46, 47, 50, 52,

M

mad, 16, 19, 25, 52, 62, 66, 128, 155

Mass, *including* Mass of Christian Burial, 76, 96, 97, 109, 111

memorial, *also* memorial card, 19, 111, 112, 124

memory, *also* memories, 61, 94, 148

mortician, 83, 104

mourners, 91

N

near death experience, 148

O

obituary, 93, 94, 95, 135

organ donor, 147

organs, 147

P

pall, *also* pallbearer(s), 96, 109, 113, 121

passed, *also* passed away, 28, 158

pets, 44

physical pain, 17

plot, 117

police officers, 121

prayers, 14, 26, 48, 74, 76, 89, 90, 96, 102, 110, 120, 121, 123, 125, 145, 153, 155-161

pull the plug, 139

purgatory, 46, 50, 76

V

W

About the Author

National award-winning writer Bill Dodds is the author of more than twenty books, a columnist for Catholic News Service and *Columbia* magazine, and a frequent contributor to *Catholic Digest*, *New Covenant*, and *Catholic Parent*® magazines.

He and his wife, Monica, are the coauthors of *Caring for Your Aging Parent*, which has been called "a real service to families."

His website is www.BillDodds.com.

More than fifty short chapters provide
practical advice for adult children faced
with the care of their aging parent.
0-87973-**731**-X, paper, $11.95, 192 pp.

To order from Our Sunday Visitor:
Toll free: 1-800-348-2440
E-mail: osvbooks@osv.com
Website: www.osv.com

Prices and availability of books subject to change without notice.

Our Sunday Visitor. . .
Your Source for Discovering the Riches of the Catholic Faith

Our Sunday Visitor has an extensive line of materials for young children, teens, and adults. Our books, Bibles, booklets, CD-ROMs, audios, and videos are available in bookstores worldwide.

To receive a FREE full-line catalog or for more information, call **Our Sunday Visitor** at **1-800-348-2440**. Or write, **Our Sunday Visitor** / 200 Noll Plaza / Huntington, IN 46750.

- -

Please send me: ___A catalog
Please send me materials on:
___Apologetics and catechetics   ___Reference works
___Prayer books   ___Heritage and the saints
___The family   ___The parish

Name_____

Address_____Apt._____

City_____State____Zip_____

Telephone (   ) _____

A13BBABP

- -

Please send a friend: ___A catalog
Please send a friend materials on:
___Apologetics and catechetics   ___Reference works
___Prayer books   ___Heritage and the saints
___The family   ___The parish

Name_____

Address_____Apt._____

City_____State____Zip_____

Telephone (   ) _____

A13BBABP

- -

Our Sunday Visitor
200 Noll Plaza
Huntington, IN 46750
Toll free: 1-800-348-2440
E-mail: osvbooks@osv.com
Website: www.osv.com